The C

is for

Complex

National Bestselling Author

Myunique C. Green

ISBN: 978-1-365-96126-7

MyuniqueGreen.com
Snapchat @CeCe_Major
Instagram @*_cmajor_*

Other Books

Literature & Fiction

Hysteria
Chaos
Professional Development
Psinder

Women's Non-Fiction

The C is for Complex
This Officially Sucks
To Mend a Broken Heart

Mystery/Thriller & Suspense

Chopped & Skrewed: The Trilogy
Last Seen
Compulsive

Short Stories

713
281
Deceptive
Repetitive
Seductive
Competitive
Minutes 2 Madness

Being beautiful makes me

dangerous.

Being dangerous makes me

beautiful.

From the Author

I'm honest and I exaggerate.

My friends say I tend to make things more dramatic than necessary. I'm okay with that. The beauty of it is, you don't exactly know which part is the exaggeration—or is that the sad part?

Maybe it's both.

There truly is *beauty* in madness, after all.

For the most part, I like to think of myself as genuine. But I'm also complex—or confused, just depends on how you look at it.

In what came out more like a diary than a story, *The C is for Complex* was my attempt at cleansing the madness swimming around in my head. Perhaps that makes it more for me than for you, the reader. If you do take the time to read it, I don't think you'll be disappointed—maybe you'll feel something.

These were taken from four years ago; I was barely starting college then, living at home and had so much time on my hands, I was certain to drive myself insane. There may be some accomplishments in there somewhere too, maybe a little poetry.

Whether it's good or not, I'll let you be the judge. It might be logical to assume that this, in its own way, is a precursor for *To Mend a Broken Heart*.

Myunique C. Green

I sit back and ask myself

"How the hell is she doing it?"

Suddenly the lazy hamster finally begins to turn that wheel and I begin to over-think and over-complicate things.

Some people just have it, and other people don't.

Well, I have it ***sometimes***.

Or is having it just a part of my wild imagination and drunken hallucinations?

I want it ***all the time***, just like that.

But I settle for sometimes.

The Turtle wins the race though, right?

I refuse to be beaten by self-induced **jealousy**.

April 7th

Speaking of a woman that I once considered a friend:

I can find no single way to describe this woman. She doesn't know who she is so she strives to be someone else. The only real friend she has is the torn and confused woman staring back at her in the mirror.

She's given everything up, for what? For who?

Turned her back on her family and her heritage. For money? For popularity?

She bases her usefulness of people on what they have to give, and if you're giving nothing, consider yourself *trashed*. Her mind is so *easily* manipulated and her body is a mere toy to be played with.

The real person died a long time ago and all that's left is a vile, regurgitated ***shell of a woman***.

Why do I consider her a mannequin? It should seem obvious.

This woman is completely devoid of life. Hollow and empty, yet appearing to be at complete peace on the outside. You would never guess the poison that lies within her complex walls.

She is ultimately the product of society and she may have everyone else fooled, but I can see beneath the surface.

June 13th

Last night (and by 'last night' I mean 4 in the morning), I went to bed with a few heavy things on my mind. I'm partially surprised I was even able to sleep at all. Granted, I did toss and turn for a while because what plagued me wouldn't go away.

So, I prayed about it.

I prayed for the power to just let go.

To let *him* go.

Which could be considered the follow-up prayer to another which I'd asked to be shown the type of person he really was. Turns out, I don't like him.

I hadn't realized that I'd allowed myself to be swept away by my own desires so much that I was neglecting everything else.

And it was ***hurting*** me.

Emotionally.

So much so that I'd become numb.

Today, I'm proud to say that I woke up with a new attitude. My head is clear and for the first time in a long time, I can think clearly and I really feel at peace.

Maybe that was the lesson in all of this. In me meeting him. For me to learn that time shouldn't be invested in people who aren't worth it. People who only view me as just another option.

I'm worth so much more.

It's interesting how it started with a text message and it's even more interesting how they could make you feel.

Words being said without being *said*.

It's also quite difficult to read emotions.

Aside from the obvious: ALL CAPS CONVERSATIONS.

With those you have an inkling that the person on the other end is upset.

So, begins my venting. The conversation (if you could call it that):

Me: "Longest 30 minutes of my life."

Recipient: "I called you, now I'm busy so ttyl."

What messed me up about the response was perhaps the order of words. My mind read sort of an attitude in telling me that since they called me and I didn't answer, I was no longer worth anymore time.

Call me a female and correct me if I'm wrong.

"Now I'm busy."

It wouldn't have sounded so bad if it was: "I'm busy now."

I could have understood that. I'd have merely shrugged and went on with my day. But the misplacement of the 'now' made me sit back and think about it. Perhaps over-think (I tend to do it), so much so that I became angry.

Without clarity, something like this could ruin a friendship. And seeing that the recipient is so 'busy' it only makes me think deeper into why they'd tell me something like that.

Granted, I do have quite a bit of a record with not replying to text messages or returning calls promptly. It's something I'm truly working on.

Everyone has told me I have a problem, I just can't seem to stay on top of it all.

This past weekend was the most stressful I've experienced in a while.

Almost enough to provoke tears.

A *real friend* would **know** that.

A real friend would realize that after four days of not hearing from me it may be time to call and check to see if I still have a pulse.

Not wait to catch my segment on the 9 o'clock news.

The funny thing is; my real friends **did know**.

I'm tired of being such an irrelevant factor in people's lives that they feel they can just treat or talk to me any kind of way.

I talk a lot but only to cover up the words that I don't say. Constantly grabbing for words to fill the silence so I don't slip up and say what's really on my mind.

There's *sooooo* much on my mind.

Maybe it's just time to just let sleeping dogs lie.

June 16th

I had such a wonderful Father's Day—I can't help but smile.

Well, if you are wondering what I did, I'll tell you.

It wasn't spending time with either of my father-figures. Probably the opposite, in fact.

I stayed with my aunt, sisters and cousins for the better part of the day.

It was such a stress-free environment!

I probably couldn't have asked for a more peaceful day to be alive. The birds were singing, the sun was out, and beating down fiercely on my back.

Another typical summer day in Texas.

But, you know how life likes to throw that little bit of a curve ball.

It appears people live off Facebook drama, as though they really have no life of their own to lead. There's always something that someone will post to put people in their feelings.

So much so, that they *lash out*.

I'm not malicious, or vindictive.

I have no hate or resentment in my heart.

I simply live my life the best way I know how.

Which is all I really can do.

With guidance.

When it was brought to my attention that someone felt as though I was "bashing" their father on Facebook over a simple Father's Day celebratory post, I couldn't have imagined the snowball effect it would have.

At the end of the day, I'm still just as happy as I was when I left the house this morning. Although it's almost midnight now, the sun is still shinning in my world.

You can't break me, because you didn't make me.

Never have.

My grandfather always told me: "You can't miss something you never had."

How true!

I've done quite well for myself, considering that I'm 22 years old, the author of a bestselling novel, and close to graduating college.

I may not be anything to anyone else, but, my mother thinks I made it. In the end is the only opinion I really care about.

I can't/won't cry about a drunken dad that was never there.

I will, however, celebrate the father that stepped into the shoes my biological dad couldn't fill and raised me as his own daughter. If that makes me a bad person, so be it.

I'll still be smiling and living my life while other people sort out the problems that they have with me.

I'm busy rising above the bitterness and I won't allow it to eat away at me.

June 23rd

Endless conversations about whatever comes to mind.

Artistic works.

Those nights are the longest.

I love that my best friend is a fellow artist. It's the love for art and the creation of it keep us from allowing each other to mess up—we're our own worst critics.

If you ever heard us interact with each other, you'd probably get lost. *Even I* think there's something not-so-right about us.

I'd gotten to the point where I thought it wasn't possible.

That someone could ***understand*** *me.*

We bizarrely balance each other's crazy.

There's something about his character that I like though. Admire even. Maybe it's because he doesn't come with drama, and *my* drama doesn't scare him away.

What's even stranger is that he doesn't talk too much, it's exactly just enough. He knows how, where, when, and what to say.

I don't know how this happened. How we went from passing each other up on campus to talking every day, or how I find him so easy to talk too that I disclose things about myself most of my girlfriends don't know.

I'll blame it on the laws of attraction.

They're so obviously missing that we really had no choice but to become friends.

Most of the time when you get male-female friendships somewhere down the line wires are crossed, leading to one person liking the other. Those cases almost always end in these friendships turning into **complicated sex** that neither party can truly recover from.

Either way, I'm glad that I have allowed him to befriend me.

And in some odd way, I've developed a level of care for him.

June 24th

It could seem like the hardest thing to do.

*Saying what you **really** feel, that is.*

It may be because you don't know the right words to say, or, because you fear how the recipient of those feeling will react.

I've spent a lot of time searching for love in all the wrong places.

And I'll challenge any who says they found the love of their life on the internet to a duel.

Because even though the internet is the wave of the future, meeting people face-to-face trumps an internet meeting any given day.

At least in my experience.

Anyone can fall in love with a set of words.

A sweet paragraph or a thoughtful sentence.

July 19th

Pride is a funny thing.

Well, not so much "funny" as it is sad.

In my family, very few of us really have the balls to tell each other how sorry we are that we offended a person or hurt their feelings. Either you suck it up or forget it ever happened.

In a recent episode of drama encrusted events, a woman who everyone now considers to be on a rampage pretty much exploded.

Just went **KA-BOOM**! For no apparent reason.

Being the most un-confrontational person one could ever meet that I am, I stood down. Even attempted to leave.

Sparing details, a few minutes later, my feelings are posted on Facebook (Yes, I'm one of those people) and it isn't long before the subject of said status is calling my mother.

I'm an adult.

At least something like it.

Have a problem with me? Let's talk it out. Don't call my mother.

Seems there's this whole "misunderstanding" about what happened earlier today, which my mother actually helped me to sort out.

Now I feel bad. But not bad enough to issue any apologies. The woman in me stands by what I said and how I feel.

The peacemaker in me disagrees.

My **pride** disagrees with the peacemaker.

So, here I am at a crossroads. I know for a fact that I won't receive an apology in return, but should that keep me from making peace?

Eh. I won't lose any sleep over it. Procrastination says it can wait.

July 21st

Just when it seems I've taken 3 steps forward I'm forced to take 4 steps back. But being the eternal optimist I am, I'm glad to only be setback 1 step—it could be a lot worse.

It's times like this I sort of feel like Job; he lost everything in a relatively short time span: livestock, kids, friends. But by remaining faithful he gained it all back, times 2.

I haven't lost everything but this week has been a rough patch, just when things were looking up.

However, my head remains towards the sky because after the darkness the sun comes out… Right?

August 4th

The more I think about it, the more it's on my mind.

Maybe this will make me a bad person.

Coincidences can so often be taken as a sign. Especially when you're ***LOOKING*** for one.

I'd like to think a sign is something you aren't searching for. It just comes to you when you least expect it, and they don't always happen immediately either. That's how they get you—it's the element of surprise. It's also something you don't have to think so hard about; you shouldn't have dig deep into your very being to figure out what it means (unless you're naturally deep thinker, I guess).

The type of signs I'm talking about are the 'otherworldly' kind. The kind where you go to whomever it is that you 'pray' to and ask them for some type of tell, that this is the way you should be going.

"Give me a sign!"

Anyways, so often what we'd like to interpret as *signs* could just be something coincidental that we use to pacify ourselves with what it is we *truly* wanted to do in the first place.

Something noteworthy that my mother told me: "When you try to quit something cold turkey, it only becomes all you think about."

Try this:

1. **Hold your breath.**
2. **See how long you can go without thinking about how nice it'd be to have a little oxygen.**

In the scenario that one is in a relationship, and would perhaps ask for a 'sign' that would tell you if you should be with a person or not, after 'taking a break' from that person for a while; it's only natural that you'll look for things to turn into a sign. It'd be the same if you were stuck in a dessert for 5 days, the sun beating hot against your back and not a drop of water on your tongue. Let that go on long enough and your brain would create something (a mirage) to help you cope.

Your mind is already on that person.

So much so that you've even begun to **ask/pray/*beg*** for a legitimate reason to be with them.

Any time that happens, that should be your sign right there.

Who needs a sign to be with someone?

It's almost as if you're forcing something that's not even there.

August 23rd

Family.

Man, I swear the term is not what it used to mean.

You can't expect unity when you run around slandering and spreading/preaching division. What kind of people are you? Or are you even people at all? It's sick. You're not better than any of us; we were all cut from the same damn cloth.

The difference between me and you? I'm not afraid to chase my dreams. Difference between you and them? They don't parade around pretending to be something/someone they're not.

While you spend your time looking for ways to look down on 'them' you're not moving anywhere in your life.

I'm embarrassed to even be a part of this thing formerly known as family.

But, I swear it's the same few that start all the problems. Why are they so sad? Perpetually depressed with life that they now only live to leach off other people's happiness?

Well, at least they have each other. The four of them. All one close-knit, closed-minded, immediate family.

I **tried** to be nice.

I really did.

I went on a two-week campaign, sending *very positive* text messages and even phone calls, to which I never got a response.

I thought the lady was dead.

Until she sent me a life on Candy Crush.

One thing that I know as an adult: if you haven't fallen out with any of your friends/family then that relationship is already faker than a $3 bill.

Life isn't set up that way.

Expect to have problems with people, but don't walk around holding a dead grudge on your chest like a medal of honor.

I wish I could express my level of distaste right now.

Stop beating a dead horse.

If you're all about 'family' then be about family.

Don't just blow hot air.

As far as I'm concerned, you're only concerned about your own immediate family and it's fake.

You're fake.

And fake things get thrown away eventually, anyhow.

September 1st

I spend a lot of time up at random hours in the morning. One could even say I have a common case of Insomnia (2 out of 3 doctors agree).

Sure, I have medicine that could knock me out for 8 hours, but why do that when I could drive myself insane with lack of sleep?

I've recently stopped believing that I'm myself.

Yes, I know how that sounds, but something in me dignifies the statement.

I can't possibly be myself.

Who am I?

Would it be possible to find out who you are from what others think of you?

From people who claim to know you?

I've gathered that I'm a very articulate woman that shows initiative.

Dear God, I sound like a million-other people.

Should that mean there's nothing special about me?

Well, of course there is!

I just don't know what it is… Yet.

Is there a cut-off date to finding yourself? Because I'm 22 and don't want to miss that deadline.

I figure there must be, since young people are in such a rush

to grow old.

Things were so much simpler when I was a kid.

Everything was handled for me and I didn't have to worry about many of the harsh realities of life.

Life can be so darn harsh.

September 3rd

There is something *strange* about us.

The way our friendship is set up.

I usually find myself wondering *what made us friends.*

It was such chance happening, I could have never guessed it would turn into late nights on the phone, talking about all sorts of **weird** and inappropriate things other people would not understand or even care to decipher.

Life is funny that way.

People walk into your life and manage to oddly enrich it.

September 10th

Ever feel like to world is after you? As if everyone around you is going crazy, except you?

I don't, but I know someone who does.

How is it that one person could possibly believe that they're being attacked and share no part of the blame?

Did everyone wake up one day and decide to throw sh*t on you, simultaneously?

And just you?

I've had enough of the drama. The only way the situation is going to change is if you jump off the 200 story building you're standing on and really try to fix the problem.

Alternatively, you could splatter against the pavement.

Those are the 2 options.

Though I'm writing this in particular for one person, I suppose it could be applied to someone else.

Though situations and circumstances may be different, the message is still the same.

You cannot run around blaming other people for your own emotional turmoil. Eventually those people will turn on you. Then, who will you have?

Yourself.

Moreover, if other people cannot stand you, how could you stand to be alone with *yourself*?

So, mend your relationships while you have a chance. At least for your own sake. It does *you* no good running around being mad at the world because you think the world is mad at you.

When you have burned every relationship you could have possibly established, it'll be you who's sitting in a corner in an old rocking chair babysitting 1,000 cats. They will be the only ones that love you.

And that's only because you feed them.

October 19th

I have not hit my 'change' button yet, and by this time, it probably has cobwebs on it for all I know.

I just don't feel the need to.

Either you love me or you don't.

Besides, why should I change for you? I was this way when you met me.

Sorry if my personality annoys you now.

Suddenly you are brand new to the unconventional, random, semi-psychotic, 10% Confusion 90% Sarcastic person—*also known as Myunique*.

I only know how to be Myunique C. Green. She is so awesome and I take her wherever I go—like a domesticated Tigress on a **shimmering gold leash**, but only because she must be.

To keep everyone else safe.

Bottom line, I think that if you don't like me, that's a problem you should get over.

I like me!

I even believe its **real love**, in fact. I'm annoyed with how you're annoyed with me, so take 2 shots and call me in the morning.

That is what I'm going to do.

Maybe even 3.

(Yes, I have a problem)

October 21st

I've worked hard to turn my heart into stone.

Went to all the classes, participated in the meetings, and studied my lessons.

So why am I feeling?

*Why does it **hurt**?*

It started with a crazy dream I had last night and after having it, I woke up with a range of new feelings I never thought I had about a friend of mine.

What is even crazier is that the more I thought about it, the more it is all I really wanted to think about.

The drive to class, the class, the drive home, I just thought about that crazy dream and these odd feelings.

Like I have been poisoned or something.

I thought about it until I was forced to face these 3 simple facts:

I. **I want something I can't have.**

II. **The more I can't have it, the more I want it.**

III. **The thing I long for most is his touch.**

However, I think he just personified the feeling.

It wasn't exactly geared towards him, in particular.

That would just be weird.

Either way, it has me super confused and unsure what to think.

Maybe another night's rest will clear this up.

Now, something good came from all of this.

I've started writing a new young adult book with the working title: The Undoing. So far, I've gathered about 554 words and before the night is over it'll at least have climbed a thousand more since I'm sort of stuck with these thoughts.

It'll be a romance novel with a twist when I'm done with it, partly because I no longer believe in happy endings.

So, I'm better off saying Dark Romance.

Maybe Dark, Supernatural Romance.

I don't know, I'm still working out the kinks. One thing I do know though, I should bury the feelings before they bury me, and immersing myself in my writing is just the way to do it.

October 25th

I'm in your head.

You put me there.

Paranoid.

Sleepless nights.

The cold chill you feel blow across the back of your neck when you're alone in a room.

Wondering if I'll jump out of the shadows to cast you back into the fiery pit from whence you came.

Why wouldn't you think that?

I have no **money**. No **children**. No **life**.

What could I possibly have to lose?

October 28th

November marks the beginning of National Novel Writing Month (NanoWrimo). I found out about this amazing month and organization about two weeks ago in an email from my publisher which prompted me to go ahead and sign up.

If you don't know what it is, basically, it's an organization that challenges you to write 50,000+ words during the 30 days of November.

Now, if you're like me, the amount of procrastination it takes to complete one book just about equals 30 days or more.

Last Seen took 16 weeks, clocking in roughly at 40,000+

What NanoWrimo has created is something more than just a way to push yourself into putting 50,000 words on a page, but also developed a community of people willing to help and motivate you along the way.

I had a chance to attend the Houston Regional Kick-Off Party, and being the **eternal introvert** that I am, I was glad I could make it.

Everyone loves the feeling of being in a room full of the likeminded, each bringing a different sort of energy.

I scored a new book too!

Can't wait to crack this baby open.

4 days and counting until I begin writing Compulsive, what I'm hoping will be the beginning of a three-part series based around 13 deadly sins.

Overall, not only am I looking forward to the end of the month when I win—and I WILL win—but I'm also excited about getting to know new people and putting myself out there to make new friends in the process. There are people who have been doing this every year for several years, which makes me wish I'd found out about the organization sooner, and maybe it wouldn't have taken me nearly three years to write my first book.

With all that said, I think my biggest problem is going to be *FOCUS,* I lose it so often that I'd start off writing and get into a good pace, then, **my mind wonders off** and I'd have started browsing Facebook or watching endless hours of random internet videos and Netflix.

If you're wondering whether you should get into it or not, think of it as a chance to unlock your *hidden potential*.

You'd never know what you could do until you try it!

Even if you get 50,000 words worth of jumbled/scrambled things that cross your mind out, you'll still have the added confidence that you did something you thought you couldn't do, and that alone is a satisfaction worth having.

November 1st

As soon as the clock struck midnight, my fingers developed a mind of their own.

I'm in the zone.

Well, I *was* in the zone.

In five hours, I've gotten 5,000 words deep and although my body would like me to go to sleep, I feel as though **I MUST WRITE!**

So, I'm taking a break from the story until later in the day and instead will tell you about the actual story itself.

I got the actual idea during a trip to Dallas, but didn't know how to write it and I threw it on top of a pile of things in my brain that I tell myself I should come back to. After finding out about Nano, I decided it'd be the perfect time to bring that idea to life.

What I've come up with in the end is the beginning of a 3-part series of mainstream fiction novels based around 12 deadly sins.

But it doesn't just stop there.

You'll have to read it, to find out though. Here's what I've gathered so far.

Tag: *What you want most just might kill you…*

Short Synopsis: A story of thievery, love, redemption and betrayal begins brewing when four people with completely different backgrounds soon find out that their vices can be the death of them.

The Cast:

Dante: From the streets of Detroit, Dante has lived his life by one simple rule- self-preservation, even if that means lying to stay alive. When his recent web of tales come to fruition, Dante will be forced to find out the hard way that there is no such thing as a

'little white lie.'

Christina: She has it all; money, cars, fame. Christina Belle came from nothing and worked her way to the top. Even before she had money, Christina had a taste for the finer things in life and the only way to get them was to take them. And she got good… *really* good. Do old habits really die hard?

Syven: A hard worker and a man of good ethics, Syven has toiled for someone else since he was 15; starting in his family's bakery. When his best friend hits the jackpot, he's soon introduced to fine dining and what it feels like to sit in the lap of luxury. Now, he wants it all. After all, he deserves it, right?

Liliana: Kids can be so cruel. Bullied and called Lard for the duration of elementary and middle school, Liliana is all grown up now. There's nothing she can't have without the flip of her hair and twinkle of her eye. During a trip to New York, she runs into her main childhood persecutor, Gary James, and isn't surprised when he doesn't recognize her. Glad to find him doing well for himself, she relishes at the thought of taking him for all he has.

Because everyone knows that revenge is best served cold.

November 2nd

Every now and again I'm forced to face the fact that I'm not as solid as I'd like to be.

But then again, none of us really are.

It seems I'm facing one problem after the other and **I'm just so sick of it!** The moment I fix one problem, another one springs up out of nowhere and does it's best to knock me down.

Well, tonight I fell.

Briefly.

There I was sitting outside my sister's apartment on the steps looking up at the stars and letting acid-like tears fill my eyes before trickling quietly down my cheek. It was at that moment I began pondering over my life and the things that really matter, and the more I thought about it, the more I realized there was *nothing* worth holding on to anymore.

Then, I heard the door creak open behind me and before I could turn around, these skinny, little arms lock themselves tightly around my neck before saying: “Nini, I love you.”

Well, more tears followed, and then my nephew wiped them away and told me not to be sad because ***everything was going to be all right.***

He stayed out on the stairs with me and pointed out all the things his imagination found in the clouds and schooled me on creation.

As long as I’m alive I’ll never forget that moment, because at the time when I needed someone the most, he was there; not to judge or tell me things that I should do and criticize me when I don’t but just to remind me that *everything would be fine*.

December 30th

I really believe I have some of the best friends anyone could ever ask for: one that makes me laugh until my side hurts, another that gives me the best relationship advice, one that keeps me focused, etc. I'm not the most social person, so I can count the people that really know me well enough to be called a good friend on one hand.

For this, I consider myself a lucky girl.

Now, I've talked at length about one of my friends and I feel that after what has happened this past weekend it's time I shed a little light on the 'backbone' of my friends list. The reason I call him that is because he keeps me together; keeps me afloat when *I feel like I'm sinking* and I may say a lot of things about him but at the end of the day I always know he has my back. He was close to being my husband too, and the more I think about it, the more I can imagine the life I once thought I did not want with him.

He continues to be the only person I can call at three in the morning and will be excited to pick up the phone and talk to me until I fall asleep. He will move heaven and earth to make sure I have what I *need* and even things that I want.

He is like my own **Superman**.

He makes me feel good about being who I am and would rather see me walk around with my hair all over my head than wear extensions.

When I am around him, I feel *beautiful.*

Wanted.

Accepted.

Not just the woman on the outside, but **the girl still struggling to find herself on the inside.**

I will be the first to say I have commitment issues.

The mere thought of which makes me break out in hives. Maybe I shy away from him because I am scared he will break down the walls I have built; infiltrate and disband my emotional defenses.

Then again, sometimes I feel like I do not deserve it—the complete love and trust of someone.

I do not even trust myself.

Switching gears for a moment here…

I am super proud to say that as *713* closes out its weeklong free promotion I have lived in a place where happy thoughts can dwell.

#1 in U.S Short Stories

#1 in Urban Fiction

#5 in Crime Fiction

#74 on the Kindle Bestseller market.

The reviews have all been great as well, with the only complaint being that it was **too short**.

Which I wouldn't technically consider a complaint, considering that it's *supposed to be* a 'short story.' Maybe it was the fact that I had chapters or something.

Who knows.

It does make me sit down and think about everything I've written though.

It didn't take much thought for me to write it.

I sat down at one in the morning, burnt out on sleep and bored when I started on it.

I was finished by lunch.

Much unlike *Everything That Glitters*, which took me a few years and *Last Seen* clocked in at about two months.

Maybe I don't have to think as hard as I once thought I did to produce a decent story? After all, I am the self-proclaimed **Queen** of over-analyzing things.

Maybe this is a lesson for me to just **let the story tell itself** and flow from my brain like I know it can.

Either way, I have been convinced enough to write 2 more parts in a short series that expand on *713*, which can only be titled *832* and *281*; both of which dive deeper into Vivica's relationship to *The Man* (who will remain nameless until after the series completes).

Though I meant for 713 to be a stand alone, I find the response for more exciting, and well, I don't have anything else better to do with my time.

Reflection

2013 was a year of *many* changes for me.

Some areas in my life were taking off while others were severely lacking.

I may have learned a lot about myself that year.

I was struggling for independence from my parents, all while trying to finish school and maintain at least a piece of a social life.

Eventually, my friends started to become burdensome.

However, since I struggled with depression for a while, so it is not hard to see why.

Having to look back on some of those feelings really help me to put a lot of things into perspective—seeing how much I've grown and lived.

I did eventually break free from my parents, and I did find the strength to let a friend, *or two*, go.

713 turned into a three-part series known as *Chopped & Skrewed*, and it still amazes me how well people responded to it.

I may have proved something to myself in the process.

A lot can happen in four years, that's for sure.

Stick around.

The story isn't over yet.

About Myunique

Myunique C. Green is a student, teacher, and author. The young writer independently published her first novel titled Bloodlines: Everything That Glitter against all odds in 2012. The book made it to the Top 10 of Amazon-Kindle's Bestseller/Top 100 list, and Myunique has continued to show her literature prowess with other titles such as *Last Seen*, *Psinder* and *Deceptive*, as well as *713*, a mystery crime tale that dominated the United States Bestselling Kindle Short-stories and remained a #1 seller for two consecutive weeks.

Honesty, Determination and Hard Work are her watchwords. A few bodies have recognized her works, receiving awards, one of which was from the Midtown Journal for a fiction, short-story entry into their semi-annual writing contest, have recognized her works.

www.ingramcontent.com/pod-product-compliance
Ingram Content Group UK Ltd.
Pitfield, Milton Keynes, MK11 3LW, UK
UKHW041838200726
13854UKWH00003BA/1207